Boxer and the Fish

Written by Monica Hughes

Illustrated by Ann Ruozhu Sun

OXFORD
UNIVERSITY PRESS

Boxer was a big dog.

Boxer ran into town to look for food.

In a shop was ...

5

He ran down the road.

Boxer ran into the park.

In the park was a deep pool.

Boxer took a good look. In the deep pool was ...

... a dog!

Boxer was sad.

No dinner
for me!

Once upon a time...

The end.